The First Nativity Pageant in Heaven

A MARTYR'S HAPPY ENDING

Arthur Caviness

TEACH Services, Inc.
PUBLISHING
www.TEACHServices.com • (800) 367-1844

ISBN-13: 978-1-4796-1220-8 (Paperback)
ISBN-13: 978-1-4796-1221-5 (ePub)
Library of Congress Control Number: 2021907320

The website references in this book have been shortened using a URL shortener and redirect service called 1ref.us, which TEACH Services manages. If you find that a reference no longer works, please contact us and let us know which one is not working so that we can correct it. Any personal website addresses that the author included are managed by the author. TEACH Services is not responsible for the accuracy or permanency of any links.

Published by

TEACH Services, Inc.
P U B L I S H I N G
www.TEACHServices.com • (800) 367-1844

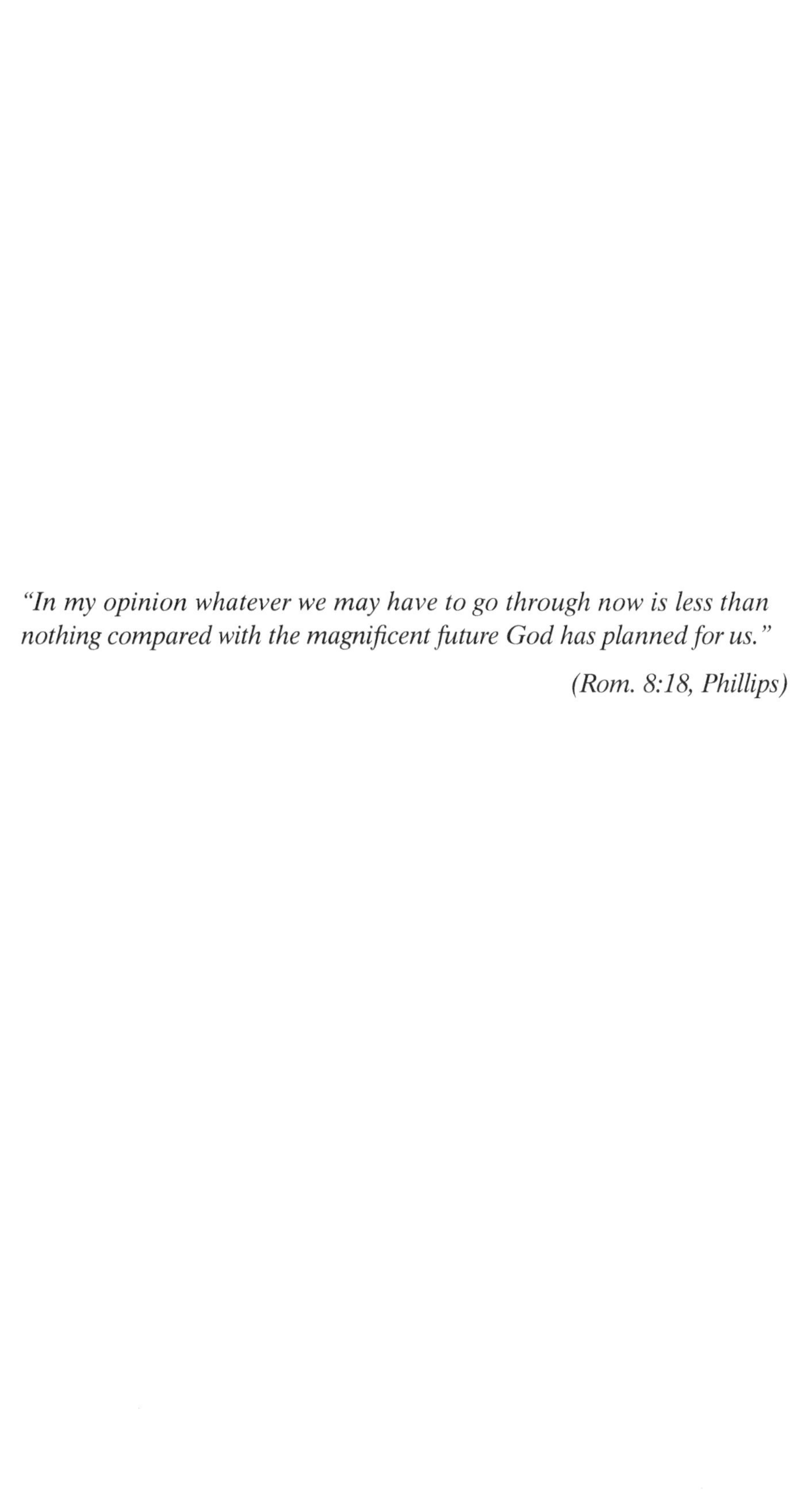

"In my opinion whatever we may have to go through now is less than nothing compared with the magnificent future God has planned for us."

(Rom. 8:18, Phillips)

Table of Contents

Chapter 1

Called to a Far Away Mission

"Very dear to the Lord are the lives of his followers.
He cares when they face death."
(Ps. 116:15, Easy-to-Read Version)

Lizzie Atwater faced her own likely martyrdom with God's peace enveloping her like a soft lamb's fleece. A poet at heart, she wrote a letter to loved ones thousands of miles away in the same calm tone Stephen used at his stoning when he said, "Lord Jesus, receive my spirit!" (Acts 7:59, ERV).

Here is what Lizzie told those loved ones. "I am preparing for the end very quietly and calmly. The Lord is wonderfully near, and He will not fail me. I was very restless and excited while there seemed a chance of life, but God has taken away that feeling, and now I just pray for the grace to meet the terrible end bravely. The pain will soon be over, and oh the sweetness of the welcome above! … I must keep calm and still these hours. I do not regret coming to China, but am sorry I have done so little. My married life, two precious years, has been so very full of happiness. We will die together, my dear husband and I … If we escape now, it will be a miracle."

The hymn lyrics, "Be Still, My Soul," were written almost 150 years before Lizzie penned the words above. The author, Katharina A. von Schlegel and the translator, Jane L. Borthwick, captured Lizzie's state of mind almost perfectly! Lizzie probably never sang the hymn as Christians all over the world do today, since the tune, *Finlandia*, was not composed until about twelve months before Lizzie's letter quoted above. Nevertheless, she lived that hymn!

"Be still, my soul! the hour is hastening on
When we shall be forever with the Lord,
When disappointment, grief, and fear are gone,
Sorrow forgot, love's purest joys restored.
Be still, my soul."

Beautiful Northern Ireland. (Photo: Courtesy of Mourne Mountain Photography.)

How did a little girl named Lizzie Graham growing up in County Down, Northern Ireland, in the 1870s and 80s, later end up in peril of her life in northern China thousands of miles from home? She would say it was God's providence leading at every step. She was led first to conversion, then to a growing Christian experience, then to a good education at the Royal University of Ireland, then to teaching, then to China, and eventually to the home and bed of Ernest Atwater. Now she was facing her summer of trial in 1900 when she was just thirty years old.

At the time Lizzie was facing the crisis of her life, another Northern Ireland native was just a toddler. His name was C. S. Lewis, and he grew up to be a giant in Christian thought. The allegories he wrote, especially "The Chronicles of Narnia", inspired millions of children and adults around the world. As a child, Lewis relished walking the wild green trails of the Mourne Mountains in Northern Ireland, and fifty years later they still fired his imagination as he wrote those stories. One particular fifty ton rock, known to tourists as Cloughmore Stone, is believed to appear in one of those Narnia stories! Lizzie would have loved to live to a ripe old age and read stories like this to her grandchildren. But at age 30 in China, Lizzie now feared the cruel loss of her entire earthly future!

"I am here with good news for you, which will bring great joy to all the people."
(Luke 2:10, GNT)

"When he looked out over the crowds, his heart broke. So confused and aimless they were, like sheep with no shepherd. 'What a huge harvest!' he said to his disciples. 'How few workers! On your knees and pray for harvest hands!'"
(Matt. 9:36–38, The Message)

China missions were largely populated with missionary couples and single lady missionaries. They came from the United States, Great Britain, Sweden and elsewhere. Various denominations and mission societies were represented, but they were united in their goal of wooing Chinese people to the gospel of Jesus. The mission community had plenty of agape love to go around, but there were virtually no single men to offer romantic love to maiden schoolteachers! So when Lizzie came to China in her twenties, she probably gave up her girlhood dreams of a dashing young man sweeping her into his life.

She was asked to set up a little school in northern China, where she taught the children of other missionaries. In the mid-1890s, two new students named Ernestine and Mary Atwater enrolled. They were very young, and Lizzie probably taught them to read. The two girls and their teacher developed a close bond of affection.

"Good people pass away; the godly often die before their time.... No one seems to understand that God is protecting them from the evil to come."
(Isa. 57:1, NLT)

In 1896, the Atwater girls' lives changed completely when their mother, Jennie Pond Atwater, died of "childbed fever" nine days after giving birth to the girls' youngest sister. This tragedy happened right on Ernestine's seventh birthday. The funeral must have seemed sad and far away from the mourners' homes back in Oberlin, Ohio. But they bravely held silent any misgivings, trusting God in their sorrow.

In the months that followed, the girls' father, Ernest Atwater, developed the need for more and more frequent parent-teacher meetings with the young lady with the Irish lilt! The romance blossomed with such speed that it scandalized the missionary community ever so slightly. Eva Jane Price, a family friend of the Atwaters, revealed this in her diary later.

"July 6, 1898. Mr. Atwater left on Monday for the capital of the province where he will be married. They will come back to the valley where his children are, and there will be a mother again in the family. The only disagreeable thought that creeps in my mind is that in less than four months after his first wife died, he was 'booked' for another one. They have waited a year and more to be married, but he didn't wait very long before he had a wife in view."

It sounds odd, but the government would not allow foreigners to get married anywhere other than certain large towns. So the children were not able to go to their own father's wedding!

The wedding cake was frosted with sugary orange blossoms and butterflies, and at the top was an American eagle and a British lion, side by side! Their country's respective flags, Old Glory and the Union Jack, were displayed together on twin poles overlooking the ceremony. The bride wore a gown of cream silk trimmed with lace and ribbons. Vows said, the Irish girl, Lizzie, had married into the tightknit Oberlin Band, many of whom had become friends at Oberlin College in Ohio, and together felt the call of mission service to China. Lizzie was welcomed and adopted into this band of American missionaries.

Eva Jane Price learned to love the second Mrs. Atwater just as she did the first. And in some ways, their love was deeper because their families bravely faced the terrifying summer of 1900 together.

The Prices and Atwaters lived near each other in the northern Chinese province of Shansi. The Great Wall of China cuts through Shansi (sometimes spelled Shanxi) north of the mission headquarters in Fenchow-fu. Marco Polo is said to have visited Shansi during his travels and was impressed with the prosperity of the region. (It was in partial decline by the 1890s.)

There were actually two mission compounds in Shansi, one at Fenchow-fu and the other in Taiku. There were Oberlin Band members at both locations. The compounds were purchased from Chinese owners

The flags that flew over the "international" wedding of the two missionaries.

who had built these groupings of buildings in Chinese style, with high walls around what was really a small village.

The Taiku compound had 29,000 square feet but still seemed crowded! At one point there were eighty people and six animals living inside those walls! There were numerous courtyards joining almost forty rooms together, but the courtyards were never bathed in direct early morning sunshine or the golden rays of sunset due to twenty-foot-high walls. Fenchow-fu was similar.

"The dragon shalt thou trample under feet."
(Ps. 91:13, KJV)

"My sheep hear my voice, and I know them, and they follow me."
(John 10:27, KJV)

The missionaries who lived or worked inside the Fenchow-fu compound disliked the Chinese architecture of the place. For example, they got rid of the "hideous" dragons that decorated the four corners of the compound.

This attitude towards dragons was just one example of the cultural divide between the Chinese and the foreign missionaries. The Chinese associated the dragon with power and intelligence, while to missionaries, the dragon symbolized the devil!

Once methought I saw an angel Peeping from a maiden's eyes, And my heart was taken captive, Like a city by surprise.

To the Chinese, all foreigners were barbarians, foreign devils! To the missionaries, despite thousands of years of Confucianism, Taoism, and Buddhism, the Chinese were "heathen"—until they became Christians.

However, just as the persistent presence of major misunderstandings between the sexes does not deter many an individual love story from unfolding between a man and a woman, so the cultural differences could not long impede the gospel's power. Once the Oberlin Band members learned the language well enough to clearly present the love story of Jesus' mission to humanity, the mysterious wind of the Holy Spirit blew away the importance of the cultural differences, and the gospel took root in many hearts!

Once methought I saw an angel
Peeping from a maiden's eyes,
And my heart was taken captive,
Like a city by surprise.
(Thomas MacKellar)

At least two of the Fenchow-fu missionaries bought homes outside the mission compound. Ernest Atwater's family lived less than a mile away prior to 1900 and only moved into the compound for safety in early 1900.

The Prices actually bought an abandoned mill about five miles out of town, which they used as a retreat from the summer heat in town. Staying in town all summer was considered to be a threat to health with open sewers outside the compound walls and no relief from the heat. So the old mill in the country was seen as rejuvenating and healthful for missionaries. One such missionary from Taiku stayed with the Prices one summer and felt her health improved remarkably to prepare her for her work that fall.

The Prices' mill home acquired a nickname at one point. Because she liked the country breezes, Eva had a window cut in the old mill wall. The local people, especially the young women, were very curious about their new American neighbors, and frequently came right over to the building and peered into that window! The missionaries laughed about this endearing development and began calling the reclaimed mill the "Peeking Place"! The name stuck.

Back at the mission headquarters, the work was hard and kept the missionaries busy from morning to night, except during a summer break and during the Chinese New Year celebrations. Besides language study, preaching, and various mission outreach activities, in some compounds there was an actual opium rehab center.

Opium addiction was a major problem in China at the time, but especially so in Shansi. There were an estimated 40 million opium users in China, with 15 million being totally addicted and hardly functioning. Opium was one of the reasons Shansi was in decline in comparison to the prosperity during Marco Polo's visit. And it was one reason the Price's Peeking Place was available so cheaply. Many farmers no longer grew grain that had to be milled. Instead, they grew poppies for opium!

"Rescue comes from the Lord!"
(Ps. 3:8, CEB)

"You can prepare your horses for battle, but only the
Lord can give you the victory."
(Prov. 21:31, ERV)

One particular opium addict came to Oberlin Band missionaries for help. His story illustrates the missionaries' methods and how the "rehab patient" lived on the edge of relapse through the whole process. This person named Liu had received the usual saline solution with added morphine beginning forty days prior to the story's climax. The solution was gradually weakened over time until there was no morphine at all, just plain saline solution!

At the forty-day point, Liu could not sleep, and his cravings were overwhelming. Those running the rehab program spent hours per day with such people, nursing them through the awful withdrawal. But in the middle of the fortieth night, the missionaries were sleeping, and nobody was with Liu except his nephew, also in the rehab program. Liu's nephew watched as Liu paced and suffered.

Unfortunately, this nephew had sneaked a little opium in with him and now offered it to Liu. The older man actually took some in his hand and almost succumbed, but then suddenly threw it on the floor and crushed it with his foot! He continued to pace until dawn, at which time he fell into a deep sleep. The God who never sleeps had taken over the night watch for the sleeping missionaries! (See Ps. 121:4.) When Liu awoke much later, he said his cravings were gone, and he knew he had the victory! This former addict became a devoted Christian and developed into an active partner in the mission program. His colleagues in service dubbed him Deacon Liu, and his granddaughter actually attended Oberlin College years later!

Chinese historians would argue that their opium problem in the 1890s was not just homegrown. They might even say that the Boxers' hatred of foreigners was earned! Starting about the time of the American Revolution, the British became the leading trading partner with China (opium from

This picture shows women in India recently harvesting opium for legal medicines. But in the 1800s, similar scenes resulted in unwelcome British Empire opium exports to China, addicting millions.

India exchanged for prized silk, tea, and porcelain dishware from China). The British even used military power in the mid-1800s (the Opium Wars) to stop the Chinese government from outlawing this trade, and from helping the millions of Chinese citizens escape from addiction! It was during negotiations after the First Opium War that Hong Kong was ceded to Great Britain. By the late 1800s, Oberlin Band missionaries were fighting a giant evil that had been aided and abetted by their "cousins" in Great Britain!

If the missionaries had understood the geopolitical aspect of China's opium plague, and if they had somehow lived to see the twenty-first century, they would have noticed a huge irony. By then, China was exporting fentanyl into England and the United States, where the drug caused tens of thousands of deaths every year—even many in Ohio near Oberlin College! Paul's pronouncement that "the wages of sin is death" (see Rom. 6:23) is never more obvious than in the illicit drug world. Whether remuneration is immediate or is put off one hundred seventy-five years, payday always comes!

Of course, the nonpolitical Oberlin Band missionaries knew very little of this big picture when they were praying and sweating to help addicts, one at a time, through the wretched withdrawal. Deacon Liu achieved one of those successes, and his Oberlin Band friends praised God for his individual victory!

Chapter 2

Blended Family Faces Danger

"Making the decision to have a child—it is momentous. It is to decide forever to have your heart go walking around outside your body."
(Elizabeth Stone)

Ernest Atwater was a leading figure in the Oberlin Band in Shansi, equipped well by temperament and intellect. His father had been a scholar at Oberlin College during the Civil War and became a college president about the time Ernest was born. Ernest was valedictorian of West High School in Cleveland and then followed family tradition to attend Oberlin College, where he met his sweetheart, Jenny Pond. She was a minister's daughter who captured Ernest's attention with her feminine good looks (only partially concealed by the strict Oberlin dress code) and by her devotion to God. She taught Sunday School at the age of thirteen, and she continued to have a heart for children, her own and the Chinese young ones, throughout her short life. Ernest and Jenny married while Ernest was still in seminary, and for money reasons, they stayed with Jenny's parents close to the Oberlin campus the first few years after the wedding. Two daughters, Ernestine and Mary, were born in quick succession during that time, and the grandparents relished the chance to know and love their granddaughters under their own roof.

The four Atwater girls: (front row) Celia with the puppy; (back row) Mary, Bertha, and Ernestine. Early in their lives, the girls gradually began to understand the purpose of their family's sojourn in China. (Photo: Courtesy of the Oberlin College Archives.)

"Sunshine" was Ernest Atwater's nickname for oldest daughter Ernestine (a little-girl image of her mother, Jenny), and Mary, his second daughter, he called "Sweetheart." Celia was the third daughter, and Bertha was the baby. After their mother, Jenny, died, and Ernest remarried, all four girls quickly began calling Lizzie, "Mother," and the Irish girl who had feared growing old alone held them all close to her heart. Their father summed up the arrangement this way. "They feel now that they have one mother in Heaven and one here, so near has Lizzie come to them."

Shortly after his marriage to Lizzie, Ernest discussed with his bride the pros and cons of sending the two older girls to Ohio to stay with their grandparents, the Ponds, in the house where they had lived as infants. A missionary friend was returning to America, so they would have a good escort, and would have gained a good education at Oberlin with other Christians their age. On paper it was a good plan. But in the end, the Atwaters could not face having the family separated by that much distance. So Plan B came about, which involved sending the two girls 160 miles away to another small school for missionary children. They would get a good education, and, like Samuel in the Bible, they could still see family from time to time. Later, during the dark days of 1900, Ernest and Lizzie undoubtedly second-guessed themselves for the Plan B decision.

Christian missionaries had been working in China for several decades by the turn of the century. Modern scholars sometimes pick fault with the early missionaries to China for lack of cultural understanding and general lack of preparation by new missionaries. For example, the common practice was to learn the language after arriving at the mission post of duty. Consequently, new missionaries would spend hours per day studying written and spoken Chinese. Lizzie began that learning process only after marrying Ernest Atwater since her previous assignments were to teach or take care of English-speaking missionaries' children.

These zealous evangelistic missionaries were bound to clash with the local Chinese cultures that included the worship of many gods represented by idols and shrines all over the country. One obvious point of dispute had to do with an annual festival held in each local area. It was like a county fair and church bazaar all rolled into one, and all citizens were expected to contribute financially to the elaborate multi-day celebration. A heavy-handed fund-raising effort took place every year, and anybody not giving had to look some local official in the eye and explain why not. The problem for the missionaries was that these celebrations were devoted to all the favorite gods of the region. So missionaries taught new converts to boycott the whole thing! This created a reservoir of ill will.

In the end, no amount of missionary diplomacy would have changed the outcome. The Great Commission itself came into direct conflict with the anti-foreign/anti-missionary factions in China, and the missionaries could no more have deflected the coming storm than the apostles in the book of Acts could have prevented the great Roman persecution.

Those who gain no adherents to the cause shall be decapitated, for until all foreigners have been exterminated, the rain can never visit us.

In an atmosphere of distrust of foreigners, the Boxer movement emerged in the mid-1890s elsewhere in China. First, it was a martial arts club (Society of Harmonious Fists), that spread from one province to another. The proponents taught certain moral principles and carried out simple religious rituals. They would pray toward a special shrine, burn incense, and chant while dancing wildly and hyperventilating. Boxers especially attracted the young, unemployed, and disaffected people who wanted to get back at those who they perceived were holding them down. Boxers were idealistic but impatient. They seemed harmless enough at first to those in authority and to missionaries.

Then a major drought occurred in 1899. Crops failed, and the young Boxers blamed the government for not somehow providing more food. They also blamed the Christians for snubbing the very gods who controlled the rainfall. Boxer recruiting material included that idea. Here is a sample translated into English.

"Hasten, then, to spread this doctrine far and wide, for if you gain one adherent to the faith, your own person will be absolved from all future misfortunes. If you gain five adherents, your whole family will be absolved from all evils, and if you gain ten adherents, your whole village will be absolved from all calamities. Those who gain no adherents to the cause shall be decapitated, for until all foreigners have been exterminated, the rain can never visit us."

The missionaries in the Shansi area just could not believe that local people would be seduced by this violent rhetoric. One female missionary stationed at Taiku said, "There are reports that men have come up here from Chili to organize bands of followers. No one seems to fear that kind of thing will flourish here." The section of China she was referring to was Zhili, which, when pronounced by the locals, sounded like "Chili."

Lizzie processed the growing rumors of Boxer activity in Shansi, just like the others. In December 1899, a young missionary man not personally known to the Atwaters was riding his horse between villages. Reports suggested that a gang of Boxers approached him, demanding his horse. When he refused, they pulled him off and beat him death! The missionaries hesitated to call it an ideologically inspired act but wanted to see it as just a horrible crime. And government officials caught the guilty Boxers and executed them.

The whole incident seemed to teach the missionaries lessons, which in hindsight turned out to be one hundred eighty degrees wrong! Lesson 1. The Boxers/criminals would probably attack only in deserted places. Lesson 2. They would not attack a group of missionaries, so there was safety in numbers. Lesson 3. The government authorities would step in to protect the missionaries if things got really bad. Lesson 4. The safest place was in the mission compound in a town that had government officials in charge of law and order. Lesson 4 is probably why the Fenchow-fu mission compound was the last place that remaining Oberlin Band members sought refuge at the height of the Boxer violence.

The previous general suspicion of foreigners fed the Boxers' growing resentments. Over time they became more and more open in their animosity toward the foreign missionaries. Far-fetched rumors spread that missionaries were poisoning the village wells, or giving medicine to Chinese people that would destroy their sanity. Actually, the leading practical services offered by the missionaries were those opium withdrawal clinics, which helped restore addicts to normal life.

At first, the government tried to control the Boxers from engaging in civil strife but cared little about the Boxers' venom against foreign missionaries. In one fantastic rumor, missionaries were said to go onto the rooftops of their mission buildings, and wave their arms while standing in the nude. This, the Boxers believed, was blowing away the rain clouds, and lengthening the drought! Gradually, certain government officials began currying favor with the Boxers, until by mid-1900, many seemed completely in league with them!

Lizzie Atwater must have heard the story of the missionary killed for his horse. Ironically, the month he was killed, December 1899, was probably the month she became pregnant with her first baby! She must have had small fears about bearing a child so far from home and safety. But she could not have envisioned anything near what was actually to come.

A few months later, something had changed. By April 1900, when she announced by letter her coming blessed event to family and friends elsewhere in the world, her fears had grown.

"We look forward to welcoming our first little one this Sept. It is so new and wonderful to me ... We have longed for it & I shall be a happy woman if I live to hold my own darling baby in my arms." That was written in April 1900, just twenty-one months after the wedding of Ernest and Lizzie. But notice the three little words included—"if I live"! Something had changed from December 1899 to April 1900.

"Preach the word of God. Be prepared, whether the time is favorable or not."
(2 Tim. 4:2, NLT)

"You don't own children, you only borrow them."
(Anne Linn)

What happened to those at the school attended by Ernestine and Mary Atwater provides a good example of the danger suddenly bursting onto the missionaries. It also illustrates the proclaiming of the gospel in season and out of season!

On June 24, 1900, an Imperial edict came out from Peking (now called Beijing), calling for the extermination of all foreigners. The missionaries could not believe that such an edict would be taken seriously way out in the Shansi province. A friendly local official told the Atwater girls' guardians, the Pigotts, about the decree, and recommended they leave the area temporarily, for a sparsely populated village of caves in the hills fifteen miles away. Shortly after that, a small procession of donkeys and ponies carried Thomas Pigott, his wife Jessie, his twelve-year-old son, Wellesley, John Robinson, French governess Miss Duval, and Ernestine and Mary Atwater to a small village thought to be remote enough to be safe.

Within minutes of the seven leaving their old mission compound, it was looted and vandalized, with even the doors and windows being carried off! Boxers closed in on the remote cave village within days, forcing the missionary fugitives to go back to the apparently friendly local official near their vandalized compound. The best the official could do, he said, was to provide a soldiers' escort to the provincial capital, Tai Yuan. Ironically, it began raining during this time, breaking the drought. But that did nothing to divert Boxers from their anti-missionary agenda. The male adult missionaries were told they had to wear handcuffs so the Boxer radicals along the road would think they were prisoners.

Wellesley, the Pigott's young son, was very much missionary-minded, just as Ernestine and Mary were. During a furlough to England shortly before all the trouble, he had remarked to friends in Sunday School that it was hard to be a martyr in England anymore, but that in China, it was still a possibility. That possibility had suddenly taken on immediacy, as the mission band faced a trip through hostile Boxer territory on the way to the capital.

Chinese Christians were being rounded up nearby about this same time for imprisonment and execution. Seventy-one such executions took place on July 3, including eleven babies and children. Still, the Atwater girls and their guardians hoped the soldiers would deliver them to a safer place, away from the Boxer madness. Back in America, the Atwater relatives prepared for Independence Day celebrations, only partly aware of the worsening conditions in China.

"Some through the waters, some through the flood,
Some through the fire, but all through the blood; ...
Sometimes in the valley, in darkest of night,
God leads His dear children along."
("God Leads Us Along," lyrics by George A. Young)

"They did not love their lives so much as to shrink from death."
(Rev. 12:11, NIV)

The caravan of missionaries and soldiers took several days to make its way to the capital. At one stop for food, the male missionaries started telling villagers about Jesus, gesturing with their handcuffed arms like Paul and Silas. One bystander seemed amazed by the spectacle. "You are to be killed for preaching, and yet you go on doing so."

On July 8, as they approached the city, 200 soldiers came out to escort the little group of seven, not to safety, but to prison. But even then, they were told this was the only place they could escape the wrath of the Boxers. They must have felt like Paul in Rome as they waited with apprehension.

The local governor, Yu Hsien, would later be known as the Butcher of Shansi, and the Chinese Nero. On July 9, the governor ordered the prisoners to his judgment hall. On the way they passed a courtyard where they were shocked to see the bodies of many Protestant and Catholic missionaries. One of those women was reported to have said before she died, "We all came to China to bring you the good news of salvation by Jesus Christ; we have done you no harm, only good; why do you treat us so?"

Mary and Ernestine Atwater shut their eyes and clung to the neck of Miss Duval, the young French woman in the missionary group. In the last minutes of their lives, the girls needed yet another stand-in mother. Mary and Ernestine, now ages nine and ten, were made to kneel with the others in front of the governor, while he interrogated the leader. Very quickly, the governor ordered immediate death by beheading, beginning with the adults. The twelve-year-old boy, Wellesley, held his mother's hand as she faced her sentence. The Atwater girls wept and gripped Miss Duval's hands as she heard the governor's command. Ernest's "Sunshine" and "Sweetheart" and all the others were soon gone without even a goodbye. Ironically, the site of the girls' martyrdom was not far from the place where Ernest and Lizzie had been married two years before in happier times.

"Little children, little children
Who love their Redeemer,
Are the jewels, precious jewels,
His loved and His own."
("When He Cometh," lyrics by William O. Cushing)

"Of whom the world was not worthy."
(Heb. 11:38, KJV)

"All these great people died in faith. They did not get the things that God promised his people, but they saw them coming far in the future and were glad."
(Heb. 11:13, NCV)

There is no doubt the Atwater girls were Christian martyrs. Before their mother died, she often spoke of the day when the girls would be old enough to go to Oberlin College back in Ohio. Ernestine pondered this and once asked, "Mama, when I get big enough to go to Oberlin, oughtn't I to stay and teach people about Jesus?" In the end, she did not make it back to Oberlin in person, but in spirit, she still teaches what it means to love Jesus above all else.

It took several weeks for word to reach Ernest and Lizzie Atwater in Fenchow-fu that their two older children had been part of a horrible government-ordered massacre. Lizzie was now great with child, and Ernest must have been hoping for a boy to carry on his name. But when their worst fears were realized about Ernestine and Mary, it cast a dark pall over the whole mission compound. Lizzie could hardly sleep. People ate mechanically while nobody talked. Their own fate now seemed sure. Boxers had the people in a frenzy against foreigners and filled the streets with demonstrations day and night. One young lady missionary had repeating bad dreams of her own martyrdom!

At Fenchow-fu, every effort to escape to the hills had been foiled. Boxers had cut off telegraph communications, so missionaries could not depend on leaders elsewhere to give advice or encouragement. They simply had to wait, prisoners in their own compound. They called these weeks a time of suspense that no one else could imagine. This was when Lizzie wrote the poignant letter to loved ones saying she was preparing to die bravely with God's help.

Ernest tried to think of a way to protect his little group. He had an old pistol and imagined that if the mob breached the wall of the compound, and came charging, he could get one shot off. Maybe the noise of gunfire and the leader of the charge falling would deter the rest. The women would have none of that. They reminded Ernest that they all came to China to share the gospel with the Chinese people, not to shoot them. In the end, the friendly local government official came to confiscate any weapons in the compound, so Ernest gave up his old gun.

"We felt we were doomed to die and saw how powerless we were to help ourselves; but that was good, for then we put everything into the hands of God, who alone could save us, for he can even raise the dead." (2 Cor. 1:9, TLB)

"In my opinion whatever we may have to go through now is less than nothing compared with the magnificent future God has planned for us." (Rom. 8:18, Phillips)

On August 14, 1900, foreign troops liberated missionaries and Chinese Christians who had been under siege in Peking. But hundreds of miles away in Shansi, there was no hope of foreign intervention.

Some Christian converts began to renounce their Christianity in the face of persecution. This must have hurt the missionaries deeply and made them appreciate those who stood firm despite the cost. The first two weeks of August were the low point in morale at the compound, but adults tried to be cheerful for the sake of the children. And the baby Lizzie carried must have squirmed and "dreamed" (with rapid eye movement) as all babies do in the last weeks of development in the womb, unaware of the chaotic world he was preparing to enter.

On August 14, 1900, foreign troops liberated missionaries and Chinese Christians who had been under siege in Peking. But hundreds of miles away in Shansi, there was no hope of foreign intervention. That same day, local officials ordered the Atwaters and other missionaries to leave the city. Mr. Atwater protested that Lizzie could not be expected to travel at her late stage of pregnancy, but his pleas fell on deaf ears.

Undoubtedly, Ernest and Lizzie Atwater were too overwhelmed with the here and now to compare their situation with another special couple forced to make an arduous, animal-powered journey due to government order. None other than Joseph and Mary had also faced a similar trip just days before the expected birth of their Baby!

Inside the mission compound in Fenchow-fu, once they realized there was no avoiding this government-commanded trip, tiny feelings of hope began to grow within the missionaries' hearts. Maybe this was the miracle they had hoped for! Soldiers would be ordered to escort the missionaries to the coast a thousand miles away, they were told. Departure date, August 15, was a warm, sunny day, and as they scrambled onto the two mule-drawn carts, they could not help but feel optimistic. Ten thousand demonstrators lined the streets of the city as the carts and twenty smartly uniformed soldiers slowly moved toward the compound gate.

In the first cart were Ernest Atwater, his pregnant wife, Lizzie, and their daughters, Celia and Bertha. Also, in that cart rode Elsa Lundgren, a refugee from a British mission, a Chinese Christian teacher, Mr. Fei, and the Chinese cart driver. In the second cart were Danish minister, Anton Lundgren, Charles and Eva Price, and their daughter, Florence Price (nicknamed "Love Blossom" by their Chinese friends), Annie Eldred (new, young English missionary), two Chinese Christians, and the cart driver. The Prices must have had mixed feelings as they left Fenchow-fu. Their two sons, Florence's older brothers, had died from illness during the family's sojourn in China. Eva must have hoped that Florence was now safe and headed home.

"Sorrow may hide behind laughter."
(Prov. 14:13, CEV)

Celia and Bertha Atwater talked excitedly as they left the crowds behind. Their friend, Mr. Fei, entertained the girls in the back of cart number one with some simple games. For the past several weeks, Mr. Fei had developed a ritual of playing with Celia, Bertha, and Florence just before they went to bed. He would carry them on his shoulders, romping and laughing and helping them forget the apprehension that pervaded the compound. At 7:00 p.m., when their mothers would call the girls to bed, they would kiss Mr. Fei and say, "Goodnight, goodnight; pleasant dreams, pleasant dreams."

Back in the carts, the warm air and pleasant feelings led Bertha to feel sleepy. As they jostled along, she pressed up against Lizzie's now ample belly, as any three-year-old loves to do when safe in her mother's arms.

"And God is faithful. He will not allow the temptation to be more than you can stand. When you are tempted, he will show you a way out so that you can endure."
(1 Cor. 10:13, NLT)

"He is no fool who gives what he cannot keep to gain that which he cannot lose."
(Jim Elliot, martyred missionary to the Aucas)

"We know that when these bodies of ours are taken down like tents and folded away, they will be replaced by resurrection bodies in heaven."
(2 Cor. 5:1, MSG)

By noon it was hot, and the mules needed water. The strange caravan of missionaries and soldiers stopped near a man who had small, sweet melons for sale. Mr. Atwater bought enough to share with everybody on both carts, and the fruit really hit the spot on a hot day. Elsa Lundgren brought out some hard candy, which she had kept for a special occasion, so they even had dessert!

As soon as they were outside that village, one of the soldiers motioned the trusted Chinese Christian, Mr. Fei, who had been riding with the Atwater girls to come down and walk for a while. As soon as they were out of earshot of the missionaries, the soldier whispered that the missionaries were about to be killed. He told the man that since he was Chinese, he could escape with his life if he left the caravan immediately, saying nothing. The missionaries had already discussed with their loyal friend this possibility. "When danger comes, if there is a chance for you to escape, you will make every effort to save your life, so that, afterward, you can tell our story to others." They even gave him a small piece of cloth with the message, "This is a trustworthy man; he will tell you of our fate. C. W. Price." Thinking quickly, Mr. Fei knew that he must leave his dear friends without even a goodbye. As he walked away, he saw the caravan turn into a field of sorghum already grown about six feet high.

What Mr. Fei did not know was that more soldiers stood hidden in the sorghum, ready to carry out their fatal orders. The leader of the caravan soldiers was to signal the attack by firing a shot in the air. Then the escorting soldiers would pull away from the carts, and together with the hidden soldiers, they would all attack in a coordinated military way. Of course, they knew the missionaries had been disarmed back at the compound.

A soldier struck the unarmed Ernest Atwater in the forehead with his sword, setting off a brief struggle which Atwater soon lost. The others died without resisting. What Lizzie had predicted in her letter home (written just twelve days before her death) came true to the letter. She died with her dear husband of two years, martyrs just like Stephen or John the Baptist. Her prayer for no lingering pain in her martyr's death was answered.

"Angels attend Joseph and Mary as they journey from their home in Nazareth to the City of David."
(Ellen White)

It is not hard to imagine the leader of the forces of darkness hovering over the scene of the massacre, rubbing his hands together, and saying to himself, "This is exactly what I had planned for Joseph and Mary and their unborn baby on the road to Bethlehem that night. I was constrained then, but no one is stopping me now!"

When Mr. Fei came back the next day to try to find out exactly what happened, he was told by the local people that, "There were ten ocean men killed, three men, four women, and three little devils." No mention of the baby.

Even though Lizzie's letter home has already been quoted above, there was another poignant message in that letter not yet shown above.

"Dear ones, I long for a sight of your dear faces, but I fear we shall not meet on earth. ... I am preparing for the end very quietly and calmly. The Lord is wonderfully near, and He will not fail me. I was very restless and excited while there seemed a chance of life, but God has taken away that feeling, and now I just pray for grace to meet the terrible end bravely. The pain will soon be over, and oh the sweetness of the welcome above! My little baby will go with me. I think God will give it to me in Heaven."

Very likely, during the attack, Lizzie's maternal instincts had caused her to throw herself on the floorboards, and curl up in the fetal position to protect her unborn baby. And unless he was directly pierced, her unborn baby was probably the last to die in the sorghum field that day.

Chapter 3

Lizzie's Hope Multiplied?

"But the seed of the righteous shall be delivered."
(Prov. 11:21, ASV)

"Many people who lie dead in their graves will wake up …
to life that will never end."
(Dan. 12:2, NIRV)

"Delight yourself also in the Lord,
and He will give you the desires and secret petitions of your heart."
(Ps. 37:4, AMPC)

Lizzie Atwater was confident that the God she knew and loved would give her her baby in the next life. But what does that mean? Will she be able to give birth, nurse, and cuddle her firstborn baby in heaven?

God is a good God who answers the prayers of His saints. In my opinion, that means that on resurrection day, either Lizzie will be raised up nine months pregnant, or God will raise her up not pregnant. If He chooses the latter, then He will undoubtedly raise up her baby to a glorified baby body and place the baby in her arms. God knows how to give good gifts to His children. And what gift could Lizzie want in the first moments after her resurrection than to have her baby either under her heart or against it?

But what if Lizzie had been two months pregnant instead of nine months pregnant? Of course, God could do anything He wanted to (see Ps. 115:3), including creating a giant intensive-care nursery in heaven for such premature babies or even nearly microscopic babies. But would He? Isn't it likely that the Lizzies of the world, both martyrs and simply accident victims, will be raised pregnant, and complete their pregnancies in their glorified bodies?

God could have introduced Jesus into the world using any dramatic entrance He wanted, but from all those choices, He picked a nine-month gestation and birth. Why would He suddenly bypass that method for the saved mothers-to-be who lose their lives while pregnant? Why wouldn't He let Lizzie experience the joys of natural, painless childbirth such as was planned for Eve in the Garden of Eden? (Compare Gen. 1:28; Gen. 3:16, and Rev. 21:4.) Lizzie dreamed of giving birth to her very own baby ever since learning the facts of life as a lass in Northern Ireland. Why would a good God, no longer constrained by conditions of the great controversy over sin (Example, Job 1), deprive Lizzie of her lifelong dream?

"He makes the barren woman of the family a happy mother of children."
(Ps. 113:9, NET)

"I have it all planned out—plans to take care of you, not abandon you,
plans to give you the future you hope for."
(Jer. 29:11, MSG)

I am convinced that the God who has planned a new life for us far beyond what we can imagine will fulfill the kinds of dreams Lizzie had before she died. During the reign of sin on earth, God has seen fit to restrain Himself and sometimes to fight with both hands tied behind His back, so to speak. But after the resurrection, there will be no holds barred, in my opinion.

Who knows? Lizzie's doula/midwife may very well be Eve herself. If they asked around heaven, they might find out she is the only one there with hundreds of years of experience during the pregnancy/childbirth events of hundreds of those daughter-descendants who became mothers during Eve's lifetime!

And after a wonderful natural and painless childbirth experience, Lizzie would be supremely happy with her newborn baby. Later she would take delight in wheeling him down the streets of gold in his heavenly baby stroller. After the baby becomes a small boy, she might let him climb the tree of life (if heaven's sacred etiquette allows it). And later, the boy's brave father, Ernest, might teach him how to fly like Gabriel!

"He will bless the fruit of your womb."
(Deut. 7:13, NIV)

"God makes everything come out right."
(Ps. 103:6, MSG)

"He will swallow up death permanently.
The Sovereign Lord will wipe away the tears from every face."
(Isa. 25:8, NET; compare to Rev. 21:4)

You may be saying to yourself, "Well, maybe this could happen. There were not that many pregnant martyrs or pregnant accident victims. It's a nice idea, but I don't personally know anybody who fills that bill."

I am convinced that the God who has planned a new life for us far beyond what we can imagine will fulfill the kinds of dreams Lizzie had before she died.

Think about this. If God can give Lizzie Atwater a resurrection body that is nine months' pregnant, why cannot He do something similar for every woman who miscarried since the beginning of time? The God who kept running totals on billions of human beings' hair, according to Matthew 10:30, has undoubtedly also memorized every unborn baby's DNA! Why couldn't He raise up a baby and a mother who died at different times, and reunite them for the completion of a pregnancy? Or if the baby miscarried earlier and the saved mother lived to witness the Second Coming, she could become with child again at the "twinkling of an eye" moment (see 1 Cor. 15:52) of receiving her glorified body!

And if the saved mother of a miscarried baby can experience the joyful return of an unborn baby under her heart, then why not the wounded soul who lost her baby by abortion? God's forgiveness for her is just as real, just as overwhelmingly effective, as for any of us sinners saved by grace! So why shouldn't she welcome her unborn baby back into her womb on that Great Day when every wrong shall be righted?

"There is a balm in Gilead
To make the wounded whole.
There is a balm in Gilead
To heal the sin-sick soul."
(Traditional Spiritual)

Wouldn't it be electrifying to think that you could be raised up—or caught up—pregnant again with your long-lost baby? "No eye has seen, no ear has heard, and no mind has imagined what God has prepared for those who love him" (1 Cor. 2:9, NLT). If I can imagine it, won't God do it (if He chooses) and even more? God will wipe away tears from "every face," including yours!

"The barren woman has a houseful of children."
(1 Sam. 2:5, MSG)

"Do you think there are more sons inside of me?"
(Ruth 1:11, VOICE)

If you are the kind of person who thinks this idea through to its logical conclusion, you might be asking this: What if somebody in the course of a lifetime, and without knowing it, had more than one spontaneous early pregnancy loss (during the first two weeks after conception)? Might God recognize those nearly microscopic babies in the same way as the known (and mourned) miscarried babies? And what if a woman multiple times took those pills that can cause loss of pregnancy in the first two weeks after conception? If that woman is saved by grace, might those tiny beings have the same chance in the next life as those unknowns who were lost spontaneously? Well, let's take Hannah from the Bible. Suppose she was not "barren" at all when she cried and prayed at Moses' original tabernacle in Shiloh over her failure to bear her loving husband a child? After getting assurance from Eli that God was hearing her prayers (see 1 Sam. 1:17), she not only had Samuel within a year but she gave birth to five other babies in the next few years! So her "baby-making" equipment was proven to be quite sound.

Suppose that before the prayer at the tabernacle that day, Hannah had conceived every five or six months for nearly ten years, but the implantation failed every single time? Suppose there were twenty such failures to implant during all those years before the apparent Samuel miracle? Could Hannah be raised up at the second coming pregnant with twenty tiny babies?

God can do whatever He wants, but He has left a clue in nature as to how He might do it! The God who created Hannah also created the American black bear. The black bear embryo needs only about fifty-five days to grow inside the mother bear to birth size.

That sounds fine until you discover that black bears instinctively mate in May or June, but cubs are not born until the following January or February when the mother is safe in a cave somewhere. How did the Creator arrange it so the baby bear can be born eight months after conception when "active" gestation lasts just fifty-five days?

The answer is this: God created the unborn black bear to have about six months of suspended animation shortly after conception. Zoologists call this embryonic diapause. (You can look it up.) It happens one way or another in 100 species of animals, including the roe deer and most kangaroos! In a bear, the nearly microscopic new life (about fifty cells at the blastocyst stage) stops cell division a few days after conception. The mother bear walks around the woods all summer and most of fall doing normal bear things with a grain of salt-sized "stowaway" the whole time. The embryo does not implant and start growing again until late autumn—just in time to produce a birth in the middle of the winter! And that is when a warm cave and a hibernating, ready-to-nurse mother will be waiting for the blessed bear event.

And it was the Creator, not humans, who planned the gestation period for each kind of animal. God pointed that out to Job after all the drama with his friends. "Do you know the time when the mountain goats give birth? Do you attend at the doe's delivery? Can you keep track of the months until each carries to term?" (Job 39:1–2, VOICE).

And for most of human history, neither Job nor any of the great scientists had any clue about the period of suspended animation God built into gestation for certain animals!

If the suspended animation concept were applied to Hannah's story, there would be plenty of room for her to be resurrected with all twenty unborn, nearly microscopic babies present and accounted for! That would give the idiom, "Hannah is in the family way," a whole new meaning! And each of Samuel's super-tiny brothers and sisters would have his or her own unique characteristics (hair color, eye color, face shape, and some aspects of personality!) already determined by DNA content. All God has to do is put eighteen or nineteen of those nearly microscopic babies into suspended animation (just like the little bear cub) and have each resume cell division one at a time only when God gives the command, "Ready, set, IMPLANT!" What will Hannah say if she is resurrected with twenty babies inside!? What would you say?

"You know exactly how I was made, bit by bit, how I was sculpted from nothing into something. Like an open book, you watched me grow from conception to birth; all the stages of my life were spread out before you."
(Ps. 139:15–16, MSG)

"No one can explain how a baby breathes before it is born. So how can anyone explain what God does? After all, he created everything."
(Eccles. 11:5, CEV)

"Before I created you in the womb I knew you."
(Jer. 1:5, CEB)

Now, you might be still furrowing your brow about women you know of who have had multiple miscarriages involving young ones much larger than the ones we are imagining for Hannah. God calls Himself the Great I Am. If you are middle-aged with a missing tooth, thinning hair, or a few wrinkles here and there, that is not how you will look when raised up or caught up! On that great day, when you take your attention away from everything going on around you, you might say to yourself, "I look twenty-one again!" God has turned back time as far as your body is concerned.

The same could easily hold true for the miscarried babies. God could say, "I am going to start over with this baby at the conception stage using the same genes I planned from the beginning of time. And if I do the same thing for all her miscarried brothers and sisters, there will be plenty of room for everybody just like in Hannah's case!"

In fact, some miscarriages are a direct result of genetic defects brought on by long term consequences of sin after the fall in Eden. It would be impossible for God to re-create and give an imperfect glorified body to a saved human being! Everything God creates is "very good" (see Gen. 1:31). So God may very well choose to go back and fix the

DNA in those imperfect babies (even miscarried conjoined twins) at the single-cell stage! Just as Down's Syndrome children will be raised up with their same sweet personalities, but without the genetic errors, so the genetically imperfect miscarried babies will have a new chance at every stage of developing life with perfect genes! And there will be "room in the inn" for all those newly re-created nearly microscopic babies in the saved mother's glorified body.

The idea of God re-creating the authentic but unflawed self of each beloved child at the resurrection is not new.

The idea of God re-creating the authentic but unflawed self of each beloved child at the resurrection is not new. Benjamin Franklin (when he was twenty-two years young!) described much the same thing when he wrote a proposed epitaph for his own gravestone. Franklin relished his role as publisher of treasured literature, so in the suggested epitaph, he likened himself to an elegant book stripped by death of its message and artistry! This proposed grave marker is considered a tongue-in-cheek composition by the young Franklin. But he concluded with a serious point.

"The Body of B. Franklin, Printer; Like the Cover of an old Book, its Contents torn out, And stript of its Lettering and Gilding, Lies here ... But the Work shall not be wholly lost: For it will... appear once more, in a new & more perfect Edition, Corrected and Amended by the Author."

No examples in the above two dozen paragraphs (or in the imagined scenes to follow for that matter) represent a claim to special Biblical insight not available to other readers of the Word. Most would agree with Lizzie. They would concur that the God of the Bible is so powerful, yet so loving, that it is completely reasonable for Lizzie to trust Him to orchestrate a happy ending for her and her baby (see Rom. 8:28). The essay above simply suggests that all the saved Lizzies of the world and all the saved Hannahs of the world and all the mothers in between who suddenly fell victim to "the loneliest grief," will also experience happy endings with *their* babies in glory. And if it does not happen in the exact way suggested here, then it will be even better!

Karen Holford, a church leader specializing in family ministries, serves her denomination's members in twenty-two European countries. She wrote a book in the early 1990s called *The Loneliest Grief*. This phrase resonates with anybody who has experienced, or vicariously coped with, the deep loss mothers feel in their souls after miscarriage. Diana Kelley, Founder and Executive Director of Infants Remembered in Silence© (IRIS) in Faribault, Minnesota, estimates that many thousands of people across the United States regularly comfort and minister to those who fall victim to the loneliest grief! And many of those have a similar motivation to serve as Diana has—her own son's full-term stillbirth tragedy decades ago!

Chapter 4

Pageant Surprises

"When Mary birthed Jesus 'twas in a cow's stall,
With wise men and farmers and shepherds and all."
("I Wonder as I Wander," Appalachian carol collected by John Jacob Niles)

"Let the stable still astonish:
Straw-dirt floor, dull eyes,
Dusty flanks of donkeys, oxen;
Crumbling, crooked walls;
No bed to carry that pain,
And then, the child …"
(Leslie Leyland Fields)

Imagine the reunited Oberlin Band on the front row, looking toward the stable scene of the very first heavenly Nativity Pageant after the Great Resurrection and Rescue (see 1 Thess. 4:16–17) of the faithful! Ernest is there, with his daughters, Ernestine ("Sunshine") and Mary ("Sweetheart"), next to their sisters, Celia and Bertha. Charles and Eva Price plus Florence and her two brothers are close by. Eva's "Love Blossom" is back in bloom! Wellesley Pigott is there with his parents, along with French governess, Miss Duval, and the other martyrs. And of course, Jenny Atwater and Lizzie Atwater, the two mothers of the Atwater children, are there. And also right near the Atwaters are the grandparents and other loved ones from Oberlin, Northern Ireland, and elsewhere. Mr. Fei and family, Deacon Liu, and many Chinese martyrs occupy special seats near the stable scene also.

An observer from the peak of the stable roof (where an angel is often depicted in paintings) could look out on the excited human beings and see many with crimson borders around the lower hem of their clothes. A large number of those on the front row (including every Atwater child) have those red bands, and the crimson glows iridescent in the reflected light of the stage.

The crowd is huge behind the Oberlin Band, and interspersed among the expectant onlookers are women, young and old, from all eras, who shyly cover their mouths because they cannot stop smiling! They have experienced the surprise of their lives when raised up—or caught up--with a "bun in the oven"!

While they are excitedly waiting for the pageant to begin, the angel Gabriel comes out in front of the stable to lead some singing appropriate to the occasion. It would later become known as "The Nativity Pageant Miracle." People assume they will be singing in the language of heaven (which everybody knew instinctively with no tedious memorization). And they assume Gabriel will teach them some heavenly carol.

Instead, he asks every person present to think of his or her favorite Nativity song from childhood. The saved of the last few hundred years before the Second Coming think of such songs as "Silent Night," "Away in a Manger," "O, Little Town of Bethlehem," "O Come, All Ye Faithful," "Joy to the World," "The First Noel," "Do You Hear What I Hear?" or in some cases, the newer, "Mary, Did You Know?" But other eras have their favorites too. Even the Old Testament redeemed have favorite lullabies whose theme was the coming Messiah! Starting with Eve, a favorite intimate family activity was to sing to the newborns the promise of Genesis 3:15. The idea of these lullabies was, "Maybe you are the one!"

All the people in the crowd, especially the mothers, have nostalgic smiles on their faces, remembering those precious moments. Then Gabriel surprises everybody by announcing that they were all to sing out loud the chosen favorite carol or lullaby at the same time! Remember, each person is thinking of a song in what the Wycliffe Bible Translators used to call the "heart language." So Lizzie can only imagine what a cacophony of sound and language is about to come out of millions of mouths. Not even the music scales were the same across eras and cultures, so she steels herself to the worst chaos imaginable.

Instead, every word and every note blends together in perfect harmony. It is the Pentecost miracle of tongues applied to the Nativity carols! Because each is singing in his or her heart language, everyone feels swept up in a sublime (and nostalgic) emotional state almost immediately! And each person hears millions of others harmonizing on his or her song!

Eve remembers singing "her song" to Cain, Abel, and Seth. Jochebed remembers singing "her song" to Aaron, Moses, and Miriam. Hannah remembers singing "her song" to Samuel and his younger brothers and sisters. And so on through the ages among those who on earth looked forward to the Nativity, or fondly back on it. Of course, Lizzie remembers singing carols with her adopted children, who now sit near her on the front row. Looking back, she now realizes that she must have sung carols to her unborn baby also, just days after his journey to implantation in her womb!

If there were crying in heaven, there would not be a dry eye in the crowd as each vividly relives fond moments surrounding Christ Child celebrations in their lives on earth. The first Nativity Pageant in heaven is a huge success, and it has not even started yet!

Even though the assembled multitude is vast, there was not a bad seat in the "house." The topography of the land gives everybody a clear line of sight to the pageant scenes. It is like the Sermon on the Mount, only in a much bigger natural amphitheater to accommodate millions! (Of course, the multitude that could not be numbered is not *all* there. Some "attend" the pageant by receiving a vision of the proceedings just like Daniel or John in the Bible!)

For those present in person, the reason distance is not a problem was because every human being was resurrected with "eagle eyes." Some scientists say that on earth, eagles had the ability to "zoom" like a camera in real-time with their eyes. That is how they hunted small prey from high in the sky. Now humans are given that feature in heaven! But it is even better than earth eagles. It is like having a built-in, thought-controlled, coordinated telescope in each eye!

Bible characters such as Isaac and Samson, who had lost their eyesight during their final years on earth, take endless delight in playing with their new eyes! They like to pick some distant object and zoom in on it just for the pure joy of it.

Of course, bird-watchers are another group who love to use their new eagle eyes. Several like to combine their knowledge of the Bird-of-Paradise on earth with their own oddball sense of humor.

There were about forty species of the Bird-of-Paradise on earth. They lived in the rain forests of Indonesia, Papua New Guinea, and also in parts of Australia. They were wildly colorful and practiced bizarre mating dances. Here is how Noah Strycker, author of *Birding Without Borders*, described the King-of-Saxony Bird-of-Paradise. It has "a pair of slender, zebra-striped head plumes, attached above its eyes, that are almost twice the length of its body. The bird can move these plumes independently, like a pair of expressive antennae."

This Goldie's Bird-of-Paradise is one of about 40 species of these birds who live in the South Pacific. The Birds-of-Paradise are colorful, showy, and have extremely energetic mating dances.

Strycker also described the Superb Bird-of-Paradise as it dances for a female "The male goes into a crouch, erects a shimmering green breast shield, raises a cape of black feathers from his back, and points his bill upward so that his body becomes an iridescent, abstract shape—more like a flying saucer than an animal." He rapidly bobs up and down, shuffles side to side, and snaps his tail. Irresistible to the female!

The birders in heaven are quite aware of the elaborate coloring of these bizarrely beautiful birds. This allows them to display their unusual sense of humor to each other.

One birder would see a tiny brown bird in a distant bush, and excitedly tell his or her birder friend to zoom in on it. "Look in that bush! It might be ... it looks to be ... it is! A bird of paradise!" Then they would both laugh and laugh. Two non-birding friends, having seen this play out with different birders several times in just a few days, just look at each other, smile good-naturedly, and shake their heads. "When we've been here 10,000 years, will they still be doing that?"

"You have made me stride freely, and my feet do not slip."
(2 Samuel 22:37, NRSV)

"People will stop hurting each other."
(Isa. 11:9, ERV)

"No one will make them afraid. "
(Micah 4:4, ERV)

Two other things strike Lizzie as remarkable about her physical and psychological condition in heaven. The surprising physical thing she notices is that gravity seems to be slightly different from earth. Walking along the streets of gold, she feels lighter and can take longer steps with ease without losing control of her footing. It is as if she has acquired ballet skills and can gracefully float over the shining pavement of heaven!

Psychologically, Lizzie has never felt so safe! She remembers when her mother sent her off to college at the Royal University. Mum warned her of vile, evil men who might attack her for money or for worse! So Lizzie learned to be wary and never put herself in a dangerous situation of being overpowered suddenly by an evil man. Now in heaven, all fear of such is gone! Lizzie has never felt so free! It feels like walking on air, both physically and psychologically! She now lives in "a world filled with God's righteousness" (2 Peter 3:13, NLT).

THE NATIVITY ANNOUNCEMENT AND MARY'S RESPONSE: A Biblical Play

But now let's go back to the pageant and find another surprise.

After things settle down after the miracle of the carols, everyone assumes that the pageant will begin in the traditional way. Instead, a heavenly curtain comes down in front of the stable that had been the focal point until now.

A two-act mini-play is about to take place in front of that curtain. Just four characters are involved, two humans (Mary and Elizabeth), one angel (Gabriel), and an unseen narrator. Mary appears just as young as she was in real life, but a newly young Elizabeth has undergone a special "makeover" to make her appear an elderly, pregnant woman as she was on earth at the time of the story.

(As you read the Biblical play below, keep in mind that, in human terms, John the Baptist was six months older than Jesus. So when the two first "met," the unborn John was about a foot long, while Embryo Jesus was probably less than a quarter of an inch long!)

The action begins in Mary's house.

Narrator: In the sixth month of Elizabeth's pregnancy, God sent the angel Gabriel to the Galilean village of Nazareth to a virgin engaged to be married to a man descended from David. His name was Joseph, and the virgin's name, Mary. Upon entering, Gabriel greeted her:

Gabriel: Good morning!
You're beautiful with God's beauty,
Beautiful inside and out!
God be with you.

Narrator: She was thoroughly shaken, wondering what was behind a greeting like that. But the angel assured her,

Gabriel: Mary, you have nothing to fear. God has a surprise for you: You will become pregnant and give birth to a son and call His name Jesus.
He will be great,
be called "Son of the Highest."
The Lord God will give Him
the throne of His father David;

He will rule Jacob's house forever—
no end, ever, to His kingdom.

Narrator: Mary said to the angel,

Mary: But how? I've never slept with a man.

Narrator: The angel answered,

Gabriel: The Holy Spirit will come upon you,
the power of the Highest hover over you
Therefore, the child you bring to birth
will be called Holy, Son of God.

And did you know that your cousin, Elizabeth, conceived a son, old as she is? Everyone called her barren, and here she is six months pregnant! Nothing, you see, is impossible with God.

Narrator: And Mary said,

Mary: Yes, I see it all now:
I'm the Lord's maid, ready to serve.
Let it be with me just as you say.

Narrator: Then the angel left her.

Narrator: Mary didn't waste a minute. She got up and traveled to a town in Judah in the hill country, straight to Zachariah's house, and greeted Elizabeth. When Elizabeth heard Mary's greeting, the baby in her womb leaped. She was filled with the Holy Spirit, and sang out exuberantly,

Elizabeth: You're so blessed among women,
and the babe in your womb, also blessed!
And why am I so blessed that
the mother of my Lord visits me?
The moment the sound of your greeting entered my ears,
The babe in my womb
skipped like a lamb for sheer joy.

Blessed woman, who believed what God said,
believed every word would come true!

Narrator: And Mary said,

Mary: I'm bursting with God-news;
I'm dancing the song of my Savior God.
God took one good look at me, and look what happened—
I'm the most fortunate woman on earth!
What God has done for me will never be forgotten,
the God whose very name is holy, set apart from all others.
His mercy flows in wave after wave
on those who are in awe before him.
He bared his arm and showed his strength,
scattered the bluffing braggarts.
He knocked tyrants off their high horses,
pulled victims out of the mud.
The starving poor sat down to a banquet;
the callous rich were left out in the cold.
He embraced his chosen child, Israel;
he remembered and piled on the mercies, piled them high.
It's exactly what he promised,
beginning with Abraham and right up to now.

(Above narration and dialog from Luke 1:26–55, MSG.)

Tell how the angels, in chorus,
Sang as they welcomed his birth,
"Glory to God in the highest,
Peace and good tidings to earth."
("Tell Me the Story of Jesus," lyrics by Fanny Crosby)

The spotlight on Mary fades, and after a short time, the expectant crowd turns its attention to the shepherd scene on a grassy hillside above and to the left of center stage. A shining angel choir appears above that hillside singing "Glory to God in the Highest!"

These original shepherds crane their necks to see that airborne choir once more just as they did that night outside Bethlehem. Their fondest memories are being replayed with multiplied impact! The trials and sufferings of earth seem far, far away to every shepherd, every pageant participant, and every witness in the multitude of happy humans.

The shepherds again hear the angels urging them to go to Bethlehem and find the Messiah Baby wrapped in swaddling clothes and lying in a manger. And off they go with angel music ringing in their ears! The heavenly spotlight on the shepherds' hillside slowly fades.

Suddenly, the children "ooh" and "aah" as the original wise men appear in the spotlight on the opposite hillside from the shepherds' scene. The wise men wear distinctive clothing and carry regal gifts, riding high on their camels. (Gabriel has already explained that the shepherd story and the wise men story are being telescoped into one pageant even though the events were separated by about a year in real life.)

"O star of wonder, star of night,
Star with royal beauty bright,
Westward leading, still proceeding,
Guide us to Thy perfect light."
("We Three Kings of Orient Are," lyrics by John H. Hopkins Jr.)

Now the heavenly spotlight starts to fade, and the wise men and camels appear backlit against the horizon. They gesture toward the sky as an unusual, bright star appears rising above the hill behind them. It moves in the direction of the stable and seems to throw huge sparks behind it, like a giant comet. The beauty and grandeur of the star take everybody's breath away. But the star is not a comet; it is a cadre of angels recreating the star of Bethlehem just as it appeared to the wise men over two thousand years ago!

The wise men are torn between watching the star and watching where they are going, but fortunately, the camels are finding their way without much guidance. Soon, the star comes to rest over the stable, and the wise men continue to ride toward it. The heavenly spotlight now starts shining at full strength on the wise men once again as they urge their camels to hurry.

Chapter 5

Bigger Pageant Surprises

Lizzie sits on the front row, transfixed by all the sights and sounds. She asks herself if this can all be true, or if she could be dreaming! What a contrast between her final dark weeks on earth, and her unbelievably joyous first weeks in her glorified body in heaven!

Lizzie's love for her Savior has never felt so overwhelming! She wishes she could find Jesus right now and kneel at his feet like Mary Magdalene!

Then her teacher instincts bring her out of her reverie and take her attention to the shepherds who are making their way from scene number one on the hillside left of stage toward the stable scene about to unfold in front of her.

Even though they are no longer in the spotlight, she can see that something is happening among the shepherds. Remember, it is never completely dark in heaven. The lights from the New Jerusalem in the distance bathe the entire pageant in soft light.

The only place it is really dark in heaven is a special sanctuary for astronomers! They and their enthusiastic students go there to view the "nearby" Orion Nebula and other wonders of the created universe.

In the soft light at the pageant, Lizzie notices the shepherds whisper, smile broadly, and gesture to each other much more than would be normal for shepherds between scenes.

They act like six-year-olds with a secret they can hardly contain themselves from blurting out! If this had been Lizzie's pageant, and if this had been a rehearsal, she would have stopped the practice and said, "OK, shepherds, tell the whole class what the secret is!" But this is no rehearsal, so Lizzie just keeps watching the shepherds while keeping the approaching wise men in her sights at the same time. She notices that one shepherd does not seem to be in on the joke. He walks with them but pays no attention to their whisperings. He just calmly plays his shepherd's role to the hilt, holding a wooly, black lamb in his arms, with his face mostly obscured by a shepherd's head covering.

Ernestine Atwater, sitting on the front row next to Lizzie, notices Lizzie's divided attention. Ernestine likes camels and wise men just as much as the next child, but she senses Lizzie's curiosity and excitement as the shepherds approach for the stable scene.

Lizzie keeps watching the serene shepherd until he comes quite close to her as the shepherds prepare to meet the infant "Desire of Ages"! As this other shepherd passes, he turns to Lizzie, pushes his head covering to the side, and winks! At the same time, he lifts his index finger to his lips. Lizzie's heart leaps in recognition! And Ernestine shivers in delight as she watches and understands the whole encounter.

The children on the front row (except for Ernestine) are oblivious to this secret drama. They get more and more excited as the camels kneel down on the right near the stable. Now they see the wise men dismount and approach the stable, glittering gifts in hand.

On the front row, anticipation builds, and Lizzie Atwater can hardly wait for the next part of the pageant! The heavenly spotlight moves from the wise men to the center stable scene, and action begins. Two donkeys step to either side to reveal—Joseph and Mary (playing themselves) and the "Christ Child" in a manger scene so perfect no Nativity painting ever matched it!

"Millions of happy humans spontaneously begin singing along with the angels, Glory to God in the Highest!"

Mary and Joseph are standing close to each other, almost jointly holding the baby, as the shepherds and wise men approach the stable. Millions of happy humans spontaneously begin singing along with the angels, "Glory to God in the Highest!"

Mary takes the baby and gently lays him in the manger. She stands there for a moment, remembering with a fond smile this real-life moment more than two thousand years ago. This memory remained high on the list of those things she treasured in her heart all her life on earth (see Luke 2:19).

"O worship the Lord in the beauty of holiness,
Bow down before Him, His glory proclaim;
With gold of obedience, and incense of lowliness,
Kneel and adore Him: the Lord is His name."
("O Worship the Lord in the Beauty of Holiness," lyrics by
John S. B. Monsell)

The three kings of Orient and the shepherds now approach the manger in adoration, gazing at the tiny "fourth King." Gabriel had suggested that the shepherds and wise men form a semi-circle behind the manger, while Joseph and Mary stand at either end of the manger, so all the children in the crowd would have a clear view of the baby at all times. Now the shepherds and kings kneel around the manger. (Remember, these original wise men had never seen these original shepherds or this Bethlehem stable setting before in their lives on earth! The fact that their story had been telescoped into the Nativity Pageant did not change the fact that this whole experience was brand new and exciting to them!)

This Nativity scene has inspired beautiful paintings and art throughout the centuries. A well-known fifteenth century German monk and author invites his readers to imagine themselves in the manger scene!

"Kiss the beautiful little feet of the infant Jesus who lies in the manger ...
Gaze on His face with devotion and reverently kiss and delight in Him."
(Thomas à Kempis)

Morgan Weistling created an exquisite painting of Mary kissing her Baby Jesus titled "Kissing the Face of God." Here is how he describes the origin of the idea: "This painting was first inspired by a song that I heard one day. . . The phrase 'kissing the face of God' immediately struck me with this powerful image of Mary and the Baby Jesus ... I started to contemplate the awesome privilege that Mary was given, being able to hold God in her arms, but also keeping in mind that He was still her baby. This cute little child whom she bore was also God in the flesh. And yet, she cuddled and kissed Him, just as all mothers do with their babies."

Now, just as called for in the script, Mary leans over the manger and gently kisses the baby's forehead. On impulse (and not in the script), Mary kisses his cheeks, his eyes, his nose, his chin, his lips, and his neck. And for good measure, she kisses his tiny toes! The shining crimson band at the bottom of his swaddling clothes casts a red glow on Mary's face as she slowly pulls away from this avalanche of kisses!

On the front row, Lizzie's lips tremble as she can almost feel Mary's kisses on the newborn baby! In fact, that profuse shower of affection is exactly how Lizzie has been treating her own prayed-for baby for the past several weeks of life in her new body in heaven!

Lizzie still cannot believe it, but that firstborn baby of hers, who died in the sorghum field that day with the other martyrs, has been chosen to play the Baby Jesus in the first Nativity Pageant in heaven! And there he is right now, in the manger, surrounded by all the original characters in this drama of the ages! And Lizzie's baby is making contented baby sounds just as called for in the script. On the front row, Lizzie feels overwhelmed with gratitude and peace and joy!

"Crown Him the Lord of Love; Behold His hands and side,
Rich wounds, yet visible above, In beauty glorified."
(Matthew Bridges 1851 hymn, "Crown Him with Many Crowns")

"I shall know Him, I shall know Him
By the print of the nails in His hand."
("My Savior First of All," lyrics by Fanny Crosby)

"And when the Chief Shepherd appears,
you will receive the crown of glory that will never fade away."
(1 Peter 5:4, NIV)

As soon as Mary starts planting all those kisses on Lizzie's baby, every eagle eye in the crowd zooms in on the manger and the baby. Just at that moment, the shepherd who winked reaches out with one hand to touch the baby's cheek and reaches with the other to touch Mary's arm.

A shocked gasp goes through the crowd as each person whispers excitedly to nearby friends, "Did you see His hands? Did you see His hands?" In this new land where every blemish has been wiped away at the moment of resurrection or translation, those hands show the only scars left from earth's vale of tears! The formerly deaf need no whispering.

They instinctively hold up their hands and touch a fingertip to each palm over and over!

The Atwater girls, sitting just a few rows in front of the disciple John, hear him repeat his four-word exclamatory fishing boat speech from over two thousand years before, "It is the Lord!" (John 21:7, ESV).

"When we all see Jesus,
We'll sing and shout the victory!"
("When We All Get to Heaven," lyrics by Eliza E. Hewitt)

"His perfect salvation, His wonderful love,
I'll shout with the millions on high."
("He Hideth My Soul," lyrics by blind hymn writer Fanny Crosby)

Now, every person present leaps up in thunderous and reverberating applause. Enthusiastic clapping and hallelujahs go on and on and on! For there, kneeling just inches from Lizzie's baby, is the Shepherd who seemed left out of the secret on the hillside. This costumed Shepherd is none other than the Good Shepherd, the King of the Universe, the Savior of the world, Jesus Christ Himself! Hallelujah!

C. S. Lewis once said, "When the author walks onto the stage the play is over." In this case, when the "Author and Finisher" of redemption for Adam's children is recognized at the manger, the Nativity Pageant is over!

The applause from the happy and grateful crowd just will not stop. At one point, the applause somehow spontaneously changes to rhythmic clapping, and the hallelujahs change to a shorthand version of John 3:16–17. In time with the clapping, they all shout, "Jesus Loves!" and then, "Jesus Saves!" "Jesus Loves!" "Jesus Saves!" Over and over. The energy just keeps building, and nobody wants to stop! It is as if they are clamoring for an encore!

A well-known choral director now jumps out in the aisle from the third row, and points to the right side of the congregation for "Jesus Loves!" and then to the left side for "Jesus Saves!" So back and forth (like the dedication of the walls of Jerusalem in Nehemiah's day) there swells an antiphonal summary of the epic rescue of lost humanity! Clap/clap "Jesus Loves!" Clap/clap "Jesus Saves!" Clap/clap "Jesus Loves!" Clap/clap "Jesus Saves!" Over and over. The crowd is one in its enthusiasm!

Chapter 6

Lizzie's Happy Ending!

"The cattle are lowing,
The Baby awakes."
("Away in a Manger," lyrics by anonymous)

In the midst of all this happy commotion, Lizzie looks over at the manger to see her baby raising his arms toward Mary, wanting to be picked up. But Mary is caught up in the moment with her eyes on her own Son. Jesus now stands in front of the stable with arms outstretched in blessing to the throng of cheering people. (Only Lizzie can see that the real Jesus and "Baby Jesus" are both making similar gestures with their arms!) The shepherds and wise men gather on each side of Jesus and join in the applause. Joseph and Mary, now standing in front of the manger right near Jesus, cannot see the baby's arms raised in anticipation behind them.

But the baby's real mother notices! Quietly, Lizzie slips away from her seat on the front row. She goes around the kneeling camels on the right of the stage and makes her way to the back of the stable. Trying to stay out of the spotlight, she enters where the animal "extras" fill the nativity scene. At one point, she has to squeeze past the rear end of a donkey to get near the manger. Hesitating momentarily, she remembers that the lamb trusts the lion in heaven, so she can surely trust the donkey not to kick her! And he doesn't.

Now, Lizzie approaches the manger and stealthily picks up the "Christ Child." She tiptoes back toward the shadows where the animals patiently wait. Lizzie is overcome with emotion as she finds herself standing there near all these Bible characters and Jesus Himself! She is especially thankful for her baby, who has come so far from the sorghum field to the manger.

The only person in the crowd who notices "Baby Jesus" being lovingly removed from the manger is Ernestine Atwater on the front row. During the first few weeks in her resurrection body in heaven, she has come to dote on her tiny brother, showering him with sisterly affection. Ernestine smiles inside herself as she watches Lizzie holding the baby in the back of the stable.

Lizzie now starts to squeeze her baby tightly, but not too tightly. (There is no crying in heaven!) It is a long and loving hug as she holds her prayed-for baby to her chest.

"A devoted mother nursing and cherishing her own children."
(1 Thess. 2:7, AMPC)

Even though there is no crying in heaven, Lizzie's son makes it known that he would like a small snack from his mother! The clothing of heaven is both modest and functional for breastfeeding, so Lizzie is happy to fulfill her baby's wishes. It turns out her baby is not really very hungry, mostly looking adoringly at her face instead of drinking much milk. Lizzie decides he really wants reassurance more than anything. His time in the manger is the first time Lizzie and her precious baby have ever been separated! That makes Mary his first babysitter!

After "snack time" ends, Lizzie cradles her son up against her shoulder. She imagines what it will be like in a few years to fill him in on his first Nativity Pageant in heaven, and what a great role he was privileged to play! She looks around to let everything sink in so she can describe all the details to him about Mary and Joseph, the stable, the angels' singing, the wise men, the star, and the shepherds. Of course, the most important part of the story will be the Special Shepherd, and the enthusiastic thank-you ovation when His identity was revealed!

Then an unusual thought crosses Lizzie's mind. She has been eating fruit from the Tree of Life for several weeks now. She has never felt so vibrantly alive! What if the mother's milk her baby is drinking every day, has "fortified" his brain in such a way that he will not have the baby amnesia that humans on earth came to view as normal. What if her son, in a few years, has perfect recall of his first year of life, including the pageant! The life Lizzie has experienced so far in her new body has been full of surprises. Maybe another surprise will be her son giving her a baby's eye view of what it was like to play the Baby Jesus in the manger!

The life Lizzie has experienced so far in her new body has been full of surprises.

"Sweet hour of prayer! Sweet hour of prayer!
… bids me at my Father's throne
Make all my wants and wishes known.
Sweet hour of prayer! Sweet hour of prayer!
Thy wings shall my petition bear.
("Sweet Hour of Prayer," lyrics by William W. Walford,
blind English preacher)

"We don't know what God wants us to pray for. But the Holy Spirit prays for us with groanings that cannot be expressed in words."
(Rom. 8:26, NLT)

"Groanings which cannot be uttered are often prayers which cannot be refused."
(Charles Spurgeon)

While pondering the possibility of her child remembering everything about this first Nativity Pageant in heaven, Lizzie squeezes her baby just a little bit harder, and lowers her head, silently thanking God for the joys of motherhood in heaven.

"I wish that His hands had been placed on my head,
That His arm had been thrown around me,
And that I might have seen His kind look when He said,
'Let the little ones come unto me.'"
(Jemima Luke)

"Adoration" (Painting: Courtesy of David Bowman.)

Suddenly, with her head still bowed, another thought comes to her mind, seemingly out of nowhere. Lizzie wishes she were a little girl and could be held by Jesus just as tightly as she is now holding her son! But, of course, she is not a little girl, and Jesus is busy receiving the adoration of millions right now in heaven's spotlight. So Lizzie dismisses her wild idea as foolishness.

Before Lizzie knows what is happening, Jesus turns around and looks lovingly at Lizzie in the back of the stable! It is a little bit like the woman who came up behind Jesus when he was in a big crowd of people and touched His robe for healing. That woman did not want to bother Jesus, but He immediately turned around, looked at her with love, and asked, "Who touched me?"

Lizzie receives that same look there in the back of the stable. She would never have wanted to bother Jesus during His standing ovation. But He gives her "the look" anyway!

Now Jesus walks past the empty manger and back into the stable toward Lizzie, with arms outstretched. The crowd quiets down, breathless to see what is going on. Mary and Joseph, the shepherds, and wise men back away from the manger so everyone can see Jesus, as the heavenly spotlight follows Him into the stable. Then Jesus reaches out to hug Lizzie. Still holding the baby to her bosom, Lizzie sinks into Jesus' embrace, which is long and very tight. Millions can see with their eagle vision the "Baby Jesus," his joyful mother, and the real Jesus, all locked in a glorious embrace. Ernestine on the front row watches intently and imagines just what her mother and brother must feel like to be hugged like this by Jesus!

Every person in the crowd or watching on heaven-vision anticipates the day when Jesus will personally fulfill each of their deepest hopes! Everybody, including Fanny Crosby and formerly-Blind Bartimaeus, can see on Lizzie's face just what it is going to feel like!

"Be near me, Lord Jesus!
I ask Thee to stay
Close by me forever,
And love me, I pray."
("Away in a Manger," third verse lyrics John Thomas McFarland)

"Resting in Jesus, I'm safe evermore."
("Under His Wings," lyrics by William O. Cushing)

"Redeemed, redeemed,
His child and forever I am."
("Redeemed How I Love to Proclaim It,"
lyrics by Fanny Crosby)

For Lizzie, this portrait of Jesus holding her and her baby will forever perfectly illustrate the fulfillment of her farewell China prayer! Instead of shyly blushing in the arms of Jesus, as she normally would have in the public spotlight, Lizzie relishes the moment, and her Irish heart sings! "Hallelujah! Hallelujah! His child and forever I am!"

Bibliography

"Away in a Manger." Song Lyrics, 1885. Hymnary. https://1ref.us/1kl (accessed February 10, 2021).

Brandt, Nat. *Massacre in Shansi.* Syracuse, NY: Syracuse University Press, 1994.

Bridges, Matthew. "Crown Him with Many Crowns." Song Lyrics, 1851. Hymnary. https://1ref.us/1kh (accessed February 10, 2021).

Crosby, Fanny. "He Hideth My Soul." Song Lyrics, 1890. Hymnary. https://1ref.us/1kk (accessed February 10, 2021).

———. "My Saviour First of All." Song Lyrics, 1894. Hymnary. https://1ref.us/1ki (accessed February 10, 2021).

———. "Redeemed, How I Love to Proclaim It!" Song Lyrics, 1882. Hymnary. https://1ref.us/1kq (accessed February 10, 2021).

———. "Tell Me the Story of Jesus." Song Lyrics, 1880. Hymnary. https://1ref.us/1ke (accessed February 10, 2021).

Cushing, William O. "Under His Wings." Song Lyrics. Hymnary. https://1ref.us/1kp (accessed February 10, 2021).

———. "When He Cometh." Song Lyrics, 1856. Hymnary. https://1ref.us/1k9 (accessed February 10, 2021).

Elliot, Jim. Journal Entry, October 28, 1949. In *The Journals of Jim Elliot,* edited by Elisabeth Elliot. Grand Rapids, MI: Revell, 2002.

Fields, Leslie Leyland. "Let the Stable Still Astonish." Poem. https://1ref.us/1kd (accessed February 10, 2021).

Franklin, Benjamin. Epitaph, 1728. https://1ref.us/1kb (accessed February 10, 2021).

Hefley, James & Marti. *By Their Blood.* Grand Rapids, MI: Baker Books, 1979, 1996.

Hewitt, Eliza E. "When We All Get to Heaven." Song Lyrics, 1898. Hymnary. https://1ref.us/1kj (accessed February 10, 2021).

Holford, Karen. *The Loneliest Grief.* Pittsburgh: Autumn House Press, 1994.

Hopkins, John H. "We Three Kings of Orient Are." Song Lyrics, 1857. Hymnary. https://1ref.us/1kf (accessed February 10, 2021).

Kelley, Diana. Infants Remembered in Silence (IRIS). https://1ref.us/1kc (accessed February 10, 2021).

Kempis, Thomas à. *The Imitation of Christ.* Original Latin c. 1418–1427.

Luke, Jemima. "I Think When I Read that Sweet Story." Song Lyrics, 1841. Hymnary. https://1ref.us/1ko (accessed February 10, 2021).

MacKellar, Thomas. "The Angel in a Maiden's Eyes." *Rhymes Atween-times.* Philadelphia: Porter & Coates, 1890.

McFarland, John T. "Away in a Manger," third verse. Song Lyrics, 1892. https://1ref.us/1kl (accessed February 10, 2021).

Monsell, John S.B. "Sanctissimus" ("Worship the Lord"). Song Lyrics, 1863. Hymnary. https://1ref.us/1kg (accessed February 10, 2021).

Niles, John Jacob. "I Wonder as I Wander." *Songs of the Hill-Folk.* New York: G. Schirmer, Inc., 1934.

Spurgeon, Charles. Quotable Quotes from Goodreads. https://1ref.us/1kn (accessed February 10, 2021).

Strycker, Noah. *Birding Without Borders.* Boston: Houghton Mifflin Harcourt, 2017.

"There Is a Balm in Gilead." African American Spiritual. Hymnary. https://1ref.us/1ka (accessed February 10, 2021).

Walford, William W. "Sweet Hour of Prayer." Song Lyrics, 1845. Hymnary. https://1ref.us/1km (accessed February 10, 2021).

White, Ellen G. *The Desire of Ages*. Mountain View, CA: Pacific Press Publishing Association, 1898.

Young, George A. "God Leads Us Along." Song Lyrics, 1903. Timeless Truths. https://1ref.us/1k8 (accessed February 10, 2021).

We invite you to view the complete selection of titles we publish at:
www.TEACHServices.com

We encourage you to write us with your thoughts about this, or any other book we publish at:
info@TEACHServices.com

TEACH Services' titles may be purchased in bulk quantities for educational, fund-raising, business, or promotional use.
bulksales@TEACHServices.com

Finally, if you are interested in seeing your own book in print, please contact us at:
publishing@TEACHServices.com

We are happy to review your manuscript at no charge.

www.ingramcontent.com/pod-product-compliance
Lightning Source LLC
LaVergne TN
LVHW052349100826
845147LV00012B/791

* 9 7 8 1 4 7 9 6 1 2 2 0 8 *